LYTTON STRACHEY

LYTTON STRACHEY

BY

MAX BEERBOHM

THE REDE LECTURE
1943

CAMBRIDGE
AT THE UNIVERSITY PRESS
1943

CAMBRIDGE
UNIVERSITY PRESS

University Printing House, Cambridge CB2 8BS, United Kingdom

Published in the United States of America by Cambridge University Press, New York

Cambridge University Press is part of the University of Cambridge.

It furthers the University's mission by disseminating knowledge in the pursuit of
education, learning and research at the highest international levels of excellence.

www.cambridge.org
Information on this title: www.cambridge.org/9781107675018

© Cambridge University Press 1943

First published 1943
Re-issued 2014

A catalogue record for this publication is available from the British Library

ISBN 978-1-107-67501-8 Paperback

LYTTON STRACHEY

O NE DAY in the springtime of 1912—a date not
long ago in point of time, but infinitely long ago
in point of the changes that Europe has suffered
since then—I was lunching at the Savile Club. I had been
living for two years in Italy; and there were some faces new
to me. There was one that interested me very much; an
emaciated face of ivory whiteness, above a long square-cut
auburn beard, and below a head of very long sleek dark
brown hair. The nose was nothing if not aquiline, and
Nature had chiselled it with great delicacy. The eyes,
behind a pair of gold-rimmed spectacles, eyes of an inquirer
and a cogitator, were large and brown and luminous. The
man to whom they belonged must, I judged, though he sat
stooping low down over his table, be extremely tall. He
wore a jacket of brown velveteen, a soft shirt, and a dark
red tie. I greatly wondered who he was. He looked rather
like one of the Twelve Apostles, and I decided that he
resembled especially the doubting one, Thomas, who was
also called Didymus. I learned from a friend who came in
and joined me at my table that he was one of the Stracheys;
Lytton Strachey; a Cambridge man; rather an authority
on French literature: had written a book on French Literature in some series or other; book said to be very good.
"But why," my friend asked, "should he dress like that?"
Well, we members of the Savile, Civil Servants, men of

letters, clergymen, scientists, doctors, and so on, were clad respectably, passably, decently, but no more than that. And "Hang it all," I said, "why *shouldn't* he dress like that? He's the best-dressed man in the room!"

Soon afterwards I returned to Italy, and his image faded from my mind. Two years later I was back in England, but did not again see him, and his image remained in abeyance. But it instantly and vividly recurred to me when, in 1917, I was told by Desmond MacCarthy that a friend of his, Lytton Strachey, was writing a book about some of the Victorians; that these rather horrified the author, but that the book was sure to be a good one; and that I, though I didn't share the horror, would be sure to like it. A few months later I had the pleasure of meeting this man at dinner in the house of a gifted lady; and though I had no separate dialogue with him in the course of the meal, and though he seemed shy of general conversation, I was impressed by his mild dignity and benign good manners. Early in the following spring Desmond's prophecy that I would like the book was more than fulfilled.

I did far more than like it, I rejoiced in it. I can, if you will let me, lay claim to one little modest negative virtue. I have always been free from envy. In the year 1900 I had been considered a rather clever and amusing young man, but I felt no pang whatsoever at finding myself cut out at my own game by a sudden new-comer, named G.K. Chesterton, who was obviously far more amusing than I, and obviously a man of genius into the bargain. In 1918 I was young no longer, and I think I amused people less than I had. I had subsided into sober irony. Well, here was an ironist of an order far superior to mine. And here was a delicately effulgent master, a perfect master, of English prose. And in my joy there lurked no asp of satisfaction that here was not, in my opinion, a man of genius. Very exquisite literary artists seldom are men of genius. Genius tends to be careless in its strength. Genius is, by the nature of it, always in rather a hurry. Genius can't be bothered about perfection. Each of the four essays in *Eminent Victorians* was, as a work of art, perfect.

I ventured to send, I could not forbear to send to Mr. Strachey a reasoned letter of thanks and congratulations, by which he seemed to be pleased. But it was not until the spring of 1921 that I saw him again. I had reverted to Italy soon after the Armistice, and when he mentioned to me in a letter that he was engaged upon the theme of Queen Victoria, I immediately drew—for this time his image had not lapsed from my mind's eye—a caricature of him in his royal connexion. This drawing, with others of other people, I presently brought with me to England, for exhibition; but I wished to verify Strachey's image, and wrote to tell him so, and he was so good-natured as to call on me at my hotel in order that I might professionally stare at him. He was no longer velveteen-jacketed, he was dressed now in a worldlier manner, which, I told him, seemed to me less characteristic, and he willingly agreed that he should remain velveteen-jacketed in my drawing. A few days later, his mother invited me to luncheon. She was old and almost blind, but immensely vivacious, and

7

a very fount of wit, and with her I felt as though I were in the presence of Mme. du Deffand; and I knew very surely from whom her son derived some, at least, of the quality of his work.

Thenceforward, whenever I was in London, I met him pretty often, for he was held in great request by many hostesses in that city. He remained as shy of general talk as he had been when first I met him. He had *not* inherited his mother's forthgivingness. He asserted himself only when he was turned to and asked for his opinion. This he would offer with great concision. He never enlarged on it. Dr. Jowett was a little before my time, but the quality of his sayings, the rarity and the brevity of them, their startlingness, and the small high voice in which they were piped, were of course familiar to me by hearsay; and Lytton Strachey's reminded me of them. Let me quote one instance. A new book by another, a rather younger but more precocious writer of great brilliance, my friend Philip Guedalla, had just been published. Mr. Philip Morrell said he had just been reading it, and, turning to Lytton Strachey, said, "He seems to be a sort of disciple of *yours*, Lytton." "Oh," piped Lytton, "I thought I was a disciple of his? He began before me." I say "piped" for that was what, in my hearing, he always did. And I was much interested by the statement of Mr. Leonard Woolf, who of course knew him very well and for a very long time, that in intimate conversation he would speak in a deep strong voice. I should like to have had the surprise of hearing that. I should like to have known well a man whose work has

8

given me such deep and abiding pleasure. Some of you whom I am addressing in the University that nurtured him may have known him very well indeed, and I wish *you* were telling *me* about him instead of politely listening to my vague personal impression of him. Perhaps you will take me aside and do so when this lecture is over? But I fear you will be too tired. I shall have to await the publication of his Life and Letters.

In his lifetime his work was cordially acclaimed. He was fortunate, I think, in that the Great War (as we impresciently called it) had been going on for two and a half years before the publication of *Eminent Victorians*. In war, inevitably, rightly, voices are loud; and war, even when all the omens are propitious to our own cause, is a tragic, a painfully astringent theme. And thus the sound of a quiet voice suddenly discoursing on well-remembered figures that had flourished in halcyon years not long gone by was bound to give us something very like the sense of relief that is ours in escaping from the din and crush of a metropolis to some dear little old familiar countryside. Strachey's publishers too were fortunate in that his book was promptly praised in the course of a lecture on biography by a man of high standing. English readers are ever instantly impressionable by Prime Ministers. Mr. Gladstone had made the fortune of *Robert Elsmere*. Quite recently Lord Baldwin did like service to the work of Mary Webb. In the meantime Mr. Asquith had set the name of Lytton Strachey on the lips of all men. And Strachey's future books were by way of being what I believe is technically called "best sellers". But, as you know, great acclaim brings great reaction. Anatole France (with whose spirit Strachey had so much in common) was unassailably the Grand Old Man of French literature, and his funeral, with all the statesmen and other dignitaries of Paris and of the provinces following the bier along the crowd-lined roads to Père Lachaise, was a great and moving occasion, almost on the very morrow of which Paris began to ring with denunciations and contempt of the departed. We are not so quick as the Latin races, and are milder. We did not revile Tennyson or Swinburne, Meredith or Henry James, directly after burial. But we did have fairly prompt and fairly strong doubts about them, and were somewhat embarrassed by the great impression they had made on us; and if we did not succeed in forgetting them we spoke coldly of them. Of all great modern writers Thomas Hardy is, I think, the only one to whom death has not brought disparagement in the interval that elapses before the justice of Time shows men in their true proportions. Well, Lytton Strachey was not a great writer, not a great man, and not old enough to have become a Grand Old Man. But his gifts and his repute amply sufficed to ensure reaction against him very soon after the breath was out of his body. I think it was Ben Jonson who spoke of "the backward kick of the dull ass's hoof". That is not a pretty expression. But it is neither silly nor vulgar. The vulgar term, "a debunker", the term that the average writer or talker cursorily applies to Strachey, is not only vulgar, it is also silly.

That he was not a hero-worshipper, or even a very

gallant heroine-worshipper, may be readily conceded. Also, he was perhaps not a very warm-hearted man. (As to that, I really don't know.) Assuredly he was not an artificer and purveyor of plaster saints or angels. He was intensely concerned with the ramifications of human character, and greatly amused by them. He had a very independent mind, and was an egoist in so far as he liked finding things out for himself and using his own judgement on what he found. Perfect justice is a divine attribute. Lytton Strachey, being merely a human being, had it not. He had, like the rest of us, imperfect sympathies. Great strength of character, keen practical sense and efficiency, for example, did not cause his heart to glow so much as one might wish they had. They seemed rather to give him a slight chill. Though he recognised the greatness of Florence Nightingale, the necessary grit that was at the core of it rather jarred on him; while its absence from the character of Sidney Herbert gave great tenderness to his portrait of that statesman. Nor did his love of exercising his own judgement move him to dissent from that of Purcell, the biographer of Cardinal Manning. He was essentially, con-genitally, a Newman man. Who among us isn't? But I think his preference rather blinded him to the fair amount of grit that was latent in the delicacy, the poetry of that great priest and greater writer. In the character of Dr. Arnold there was such a wealth of grit, and a strenuousness so terrific that one may rather wonder how Strachey could bear to think of him and write of him. The portrait fails, I think, because it is composed throughout in a vein of sheer mockery. It is the only work of his that does not seek, does not hesitate, does not penetrate, and is definitely unfair. It is the only work of his that might, so far as it goes, justify the application to him of that term which shall not again soil my lips and afflict your ears.

The vein of mockery was very strong in him certainly, and constantly asserted itself in his writings. A satirist he was not. Mockery is a light and lambent, rather irresponsible thing. "*On se moque de ce qu'on aime*" is a true saying. Strachey was always ready to mock what he loved. In mockery there is no malice. In satire there may be plenty of it. Pope was full of it. But he was rather an exception. Your satirist is mostly a robust fellow, as was Aristophanes, as were Juvenal and Swift; a fellow laying about him lustily, for the purpose of hurting, of injuring people who, in his opinion, ought to be hurt and injured. He may, like Aristophanes, have an abundant, a glorious gift for mockery. But fundamentally he is grim. He is grimly concerned with what he hates in the age to which he belongs. I do not remember having found anywhere in the works of Lytton Strachey one passing reference to any current event. He was quite definitely, and quite impenitently, what in current jargon is called an escapist.

Need we be angry? It takes all kinds to make a world, or even to make a national literature. Even for spirits less fastidious than Strachey's, there is, even at the best of times, a great charm in the past. Time, that sedulous artist, has been at work on it, selecting and rejecting with great tact. The past is a work of art, free from irrelevancies and loose ends. There are, for our vision, comparatively few people in it, and all of them are interesting people. The dullards have all disappeared—all but those whose dullness was so pronounced as to be in itself for us an amusing virtue. And in the past there is so blessedly nothing for us to worry about. Everything is settled. There's nothing to be done about it—nothing but to contemplate it and blandly form theories about this or that aspect of it. Strachey was by temperament an Eighteenth Century man. In the Age of Reason, and of Wit too, he felt far more at home than in the aftermath of the Industrial Revolution, and in the first fine careless rapture of the Internal Combustion Engine. Even we, in spite of our coarseness, deplore these great phenomena, and wish they had never happened, and grieve that mankind will not in any foreseeable future be able to shake them off and be quit of them. Strachey, like the good Eighteenth Century Englishman that he was, had close contacts with France. Indeed I feel that he was even more at ease in French than in English literature and life. It was in that handbook on French literature that he made his début. In the volume entitled *Books and Characters* (published in 1922) and in his last work, *Portraits in Miniature* (1931), there is constant truancy to France. Racine, Voltaire, Rousseau, Mme. de Sévigné, the Abbé Morellet, Mme. du Deffand, the Président de Brosses—with all of these he is on terms of cosiest intimacy. To our native Victorians he was rather in the relation of a visitor, an inquirer, an inquisitor. I don't think he was—as Desmond MacCarthy had gathered from him that he was—"horrified" by them. He disliked the nineteenth century in comparison with its forerunner, but it appealed to him far more than could the twentieth. Machinery, science and applied science, had not yet got a really firm grip on England, and moreover, in spite of one Reform Bill after another, government was still oligarchic. Inequality flourished almost as much as ever. Barriers were almost as ever high. The seeds of standardisation and of mass-production had not been even sown. Life was full of salient variety, of idiosyncracy, of oddity, of character, character untrammelled. Giles Lytton Strachey (I feel that I ought to have said this at the outset) was born on March the first, 1880. And therefore, when, in his maturity, he began to write about the Victorians he was old enough to know his way about and among them, having been nurtured among elders to whom they were familiar; and he was young enough to feel far away from them, to be curious about them, to be wondering at them greatly. The immediate past, the time that one almost belongs to—almost but not quite—is peculiarly tantalising. Perhaps Strachey was rather ashamed of the hold the Victorians had on him in virtue of their proximity. And perhaps it was for this reason, and to shake off these insidious rivals to his dear ones of the Eighteenth Century, or perhaps it was merely in a sudden spirit of adventure, that he plunged off into the court of Queen Elizabeth. Anyway it was a brave thing to do. *Elizabeth and Essex* (published in 1928) is a finely constructed work, but seems to me to be essentially guess-work. A very robustious, slapdash writer might convince me that he was in close touch with the souls of those beings whose actions and motives are to me as mysterious as those of wild animals in an impenetrable jungle. You rightly infer that I am *not* a Sixteenth Century man. And I make so bold as to say "Neither was Lytton Strachey."

"A finely constructed work" I have said. But what work of Lytton Strachey's, large or small, was not admirably firm in structure?—*totus, teres atque rotundus.* I make no apology for that tag: it is so often forgotten by gifted authors. Let us not ignore the virtue of form in literature. It is the goblet for the wine. Be the wine never so good, is not our enjoyment of it diminished if the hospitable vintner pours it forth to be lapped up by us from the ground with our tongues? Improvisation is the essence of good talk. Heaven defend us from the talker who doles out things prepared for us! But let heaven not less defend us from the beautifully spontaneous writer who puts his trust in the inspiration of the moment!—unless indeed he be a man of genius, of genius that creates for him a rough but sufficing form in his wild career. No writer need despise literary form as something artificial and unworthy of him. Nature herself, with her flowers and her trees, with many of her hills and streams and valleys, even with some of her human beings, is an ardent and unashamed formalist. I would advise any young writer—or any middle-aged or old one who may be needing advice—to think out carefully, before he begins his novel, or biography, or essay, or what not, the shape that it should have. I would say to him—quoting another excellent Horatian tag—*Respice finem.* Let him before he begins know just how he is going to end. And I would, at the risk of boring him, insist that the beginning is not less important than the end, and that what comes between them is no less important than they. In journalism, I have often been told, the first sentence is the thing that matters most. Grip the reader's attention, and all will be well. I am not sure that this is so. Not long before the outbreak of war, when paper was very plentiful, I saw in an evening paper a signed article about Karl Marx. The first sentence was as follows: "Deep down in a grave at Highgate the corpse of Karl Marx lies rotting." So far, so good. But what followed was a quite mild and well-reasoned depreciation of that writer's doctrines. The average reader, the man in the street, had been gripped only to be disappointed. Well, literature is not read in the street. Streets are not what they were when Thomas Macaulay would walk from the Albany to Clapham Common reading Sophocles all the way. Literature is read in homes only, and I fancy that in those quiet surroundings the reader of it should at the outset be rather invited, engaged, allured, than gripped. Indeed, I think you will find that in all periods good poets or writers of prose have, whether in long or in short works, made quiet beginnings. Quiet endings, too. The reader, they have all instinctively felt, should be lifted gently out of himself, and borne up and up, and along, and in due course be set down gently, to remember his adventure.

Strachey, certainly, had this good instinct, and obeyed it always. James Boswell, describing the conversation of members of The Club, recorded the delight of watching Edmund Burke "winding himself like a serpent into his subject". Even so was Strachey wont to wind himself into his subject—and eventually out of it—suavely. Let me quote, as an instance, the opening and the closing words of the essay on the Abbé Morellet (a disciple of Diderot, a favoured friend of Madame Helvétius, and at one time a quite well-treated prisoner in the Bastille):

"Talleyrand once remarked that only those who had lived in France before the Revolution had really experienced *la douceur de vivre*. The Abbé Morellet would have agreed with him. Born in 1727 at Lyons, the son of a small paper merchant, how was it possible, in that age of caste and privilege, that André Morellet should have known anything of life but what was hard, dull, and insignificant?"

Then comes the tale of the Abbé's career, beautifully told, and concluding with this picture of his old age, when he used to sit dozing by the fire in the drawing-room of young Madame de Rémusat:

"He was treated with great respect by everybody; even the First Consul was flattering; even the Emperor was polite, and made him a Senator. Then the Emperor disappeared, and a Bourbon ruled on the throne of his fathers. With that tenacity of life which seems to have been the portion of the creatures of the eighteenth century, Morellet continued in this world until his ninety-second year. But this world was no longer what it used to be: something had gone wrong. Those agitations, those arrangements and rearrangements, they seemed hardly worth attending to. One might as well doze. All his young friends were very kind certainly, but did they understand? How could they? What had been their experience of life? As for him, ah! *he* had listened to Diderot—used to sit for hours talking in the Tuileries Gardens with D'Alembert and Mademoiselle de Lespinasse—mentioned by Voltaire—spent half a life-time at Auteuil with dear Madame Helvétius—imprisoned in the Bastille...he nodded. Yes! *He* had known *la douceur de vivre*."

Exquisitely beautiful, that diminuendo, is it not? And as tender as it is profound. I have said that Strachey was not, for aught I knew, a warm-hearted man. A tender-hearted man he assuredly was.

As biographer, he had, besides his gift for construction, the advantage of a splendid gift for narrative. He was a masterly teller of tales, long or short, tragic or comic. He could, as it were, *see* the thing he had to tell, *see* the people concerned in it, see them outwardly and inwardly, and make us share gratefully his vision. Who could have made so much as he of such things as the adventures of "the boy Jones" in Buckingham Palace, of the inception and the building of the Albert Memorial, of Mr. Gorham's vicissitudes in the Court of Arches and the Judicial Committee of the Privy Council? As the finest example of his narrative gift—I had almost said his dramatic gift—I would choose perhaps his treatment of what led to the tragedy of the dereliction and death of General Gordon. The tremendous tale, charged with the strangely diverse characters of the eminent men involved in it—Gladstone, Hartington, Baring, and Gordon himself—is told with the subtlest strength, oscillating steadily, with the swing of a pendulum, between Downing Street and the Soudan. For a while we are in the one place, then we are with equal vividness in the other, alternately, repeatedly; and great is the cumulative effect of this prolonged strophe and antistrophe. To those of you who are, as I am, fond of thrills, but have never read these pages, I would say earnestly, "Read these pages."

The element of criticism was implicit, and often explicit, in all Lytton Strachey's biographical work. From time to time he indulged in criticism undiluted. As a literary critic alone he would have been worthy to be remembered. The best kind of critic—the helpfully interpretative, the almost creative critic—is very passive before he becomes active. Such an one was Strachey. With an intellect of steely quality there was combined in him a deep sensibility and receptivity. He had felt before he thought. And two at least of his critical works—his long essay on Racine, and his Leslie Stephen Lecture on Pope—happened to be of cardinal, of crucial effect. Racine had never had high repute upon these shores; and the Romantic Movement had reduced Pope to a small shadow among our own poets. It was Strachey's silver trumpet that woke the young men of two decades ago to high appreciation of those two worthies. And by the way, literature apart, aren't there in the Elysian Fields two other worthies who have reason to be grateful to the supposed iconoclast?—Queen Victoria and the Prince Consort? The Prince in his life-time had never been popular; and after Sir Theodore Martin's saccharine biography he had become a veritable mock. I never heard a kind word for him. The Queen, who in my childhood and youth had been not only revered but worshipped, was, soon after her death, no longer in public favour. Her faults had become known, and her virtues were unheeded. This is not so now; and is not so by reason of Lytton Strachey's fully judicial presentment of her with all the faults over which her virtues so very much preponderated. And it is, by the same token, through him that we know the Prince not as just dreadfully admirable, but as some one to be loved and to be sorry for.

But after all—and perhaps you are saying "Oh, if only it *were* all!"—it is as a writer, in the strict sense, as a user of that very beautiful medium, the English language, that I would especially extol Lytton Strachey. There is such a word as *prosaist*. It is a word that we never use; whereas *prosateur* is not seldom on the lips of Frenchmen, and is spoken in a very serious tone, a tone as serious as that in which we use the word *poet*. Frenchmen are keenly aware of the virtues of prose, and we, not being so, have accepted the idea that French prose is superior to ours. Undoubtedly, the general level of it is so. The average Frenchman writes better prose than the average Englishman. His medium is a language whose greatly prevailing Latinity makes it far more lucid than ours. It is, moreover, a language that has been by authority kept free from corruption. We have had no Richelieu, and if we had we would not, in our sturdy independence, have bowed down to the mandarins of his creation. Our prosaists, to achieve lucidity and euphony, have to do a good deal of filtration on the way. I remember Lytton Strachey once said to me, in reference to this need, that he wished he were a Frenchman, writing in French. I rather shocked him by saying "Oh, any fool can write good French prose." But truth is in itself so good a thing that one may be pardoned for exaggerating it every now and then. Good English is, I am sure, far less easy to write than good French; and "*pour être difficile la tâche n'est que plus glorieuse*"; and difficulties surmounted (though only had they not been surmounted would the reader be conscious of them) do somehow, I am convinced, enrich the texture of good writing. The English language, being part Latin, part Saxon, is, in my rough insular opinion, an even finer medium than the French one. Latin is, one might say, its bony structure, Saxon its flesh and blood. And of these two Latin is perhaps the more important. A skeleton by itself is a noble thing, whereas an inchoate mass of flesh and blood is not. A writer who has not in boyhood been well-grounded in Latin is at a grievous disadvantage. However keen a natural instinct he may have for writing, he will be diffuse, he will be sloppy, as was, for example, D.H. Lawrence, whose prose was so dangerous a model for young admirers of his philosophy. The Latin element, on the other hand, should not have too strong a hold on a writer, leading him to over-great austerity and nobility, even to aridity, as happened so often in the seventeenth and eighteenth centuries. In the best writing neither element prevails. The two merge indistinguishably in each other.

To single Lytton Strachey out as a born writer would be to offend a great number of people. For there is a very widespread and comfortable belief that we are all of us born writers. Not long ago I heard that agile and mellifluous quodlibetarian, Dr. Joad, saying in answer to a questioner who wanted to write good letters, that anybody could write good letters: one had but to think out clearly what one wanted to say, and then set it down in the simplest terms. And a few weeks later, when the writing of books was under discussion, he said that the writers who thought most about how they should write were the hardest to read; and again he seemed to think lucidity all-sufficing. I admit that Herbert Spencer had also, many years ago, seemed to think so, and said so. But I maintain that had he not thought so, had Nature at the outset endowed him fully with a gift for writing, we should all of us be now reading him with greater zest and constancy than we do. A true gift for writing, though in spite of the telephone we all do still write letters sometimes, and though authors of books are more than ever numerous, is not widely bestowed. Nor is a true gift for painting, or for playing the violin; and of that we are somehow aware. We do not say to a violinist "Just think out clearly what you want to express and then go straight ahead. Never mind how you handle your bow," nor to a painter, "Got your subject and your scheme of colour in your head all right, eh? Then don't bother about how you lay your paints on, dear old boy." Let us not make similar remarks to writers. I am willing to concede that in the eighteen-nineties perhaps rather too much thought was given to *manner* in literature. The young men of that decade were perhaps over-influenced by the example of such elders as Walter Pater and Robert Louis Stevenson, over-fond of unusual words and peculiar cadences. Preciosity is a fault on the right side; but it is a fault. A venial one? Yes, in Pater, the essayist. But not in Stevenson, the novelist, when he was telling a straightforward story and wishing to give the reader an illusion of reality. From such books as *Treasure Island* and *The Master of Ballantrae* I have never for one moment had that illusion, have been too acutely and delightedly conscious of the technical graces and ingenuities of the author. When Stevenson did not aim at realism, and was entirely oblivious of Sir Walter Scott, and was giving rein to his own riotous sense of fantasy, as in *The New Arabian Nights*, or *The Dynamiter*, or *The Wrong Box*, the jewelled elaboration of the manner becomes an integral part of the fun, and keeps us laughing the more irresistibly and the more loudly. These books are, I think, far and away his best—the most characteristic of himself, of his true and magical self. I have always regretted that Maurice Hewlett, one of the lights of the 'nineties and of later years, was not a humourist and wished to illude us with his tales; for his preciosity was fatal to his wish. Besides, it was a robust preciosity; and that is unnatural, is a contradiction in terms.

I conceive that had Lytton Strachey been a young man in those 'nineties, and not the merely growing boy that he was in most of them, he might have inclined to preciosity. Of this you will find no jot in his prose. His manner, though classical, is entirely natural, and rather shy. He makes no attempt to dazzle. He is not even afraid of clichés. He can be very homely. When he is narrating something humdrum he is quite congruously pedestrian; though even then felicities are apt to come shining forth by the way; as, for instance, in his account of how the young Queen Victoria's popularity was restored by the happiness of her marriage.

> "The middle classes, in particular, were pleased. They liked a love-match; they liked a household in which they seemed to see reflected as in some resplendent looking-glass, the ideal image of the very lives they lived themselves. Their own existences, less exalted, but oh! so soothingly similar, acquired an added excellence, an added succulence, from the early hours, the regularity, the plain tuckers, the round games, the roast beef and Yorkshire pudding of Osborne."

His manner is infinitely flexible, in accord to every variation of whatever his theme may be. Consider the differences between his ways of writing about Lord Melbourne, Lord Palmerston, Mr. Disraeli, and Mr. Gladstone. His manner seems to bring us into the very presence of these widely disparate Premiers. Note the mellow and leisurely be-nignity of the cadences in which he writes of Lord Melbourne—"the autumn rose," as he called him. Note the sharp brisk straightforward buoyancy of the writing whenever Lord Palmerston appears; and the elaborate Oriental richness of manner when Mr. Disraeli is on the scene. And does not all the subtlety of Mr. Gladstone confront us when we are asked, "What, then, was the truth? In the physical universe there are no chimeras. But man is more various than nature; was Mr. Gladstone perhaps a chimera of the spirit? Did his very essence lie in the confusion of incompatibles? His very essence? It eludes the hand that grasps it. One is baffled, as his political opponents were fifty years ago. The soft serpent coils harden into quick strength that has vanished, leaving only emptiness and perplexity behind." I can't help repeating to you the first words of that last sentence. "The soft serpent coils harden into quick strength that has vanished." Was ever speed so well suggested as in those eleven words? —words of a born writer, and a taker, we may be sure, of infinite pains.

If I were asked what seemed to me the paramount quality of Lytton Strachey's prose, I should reply, in one word, Beauty. That is perhaps a rather old-fashioned word, a word jarring to young writers, and to young painters or musicians, and by them associated with folly, with vanity and frivolity. To me it is still a noble word, and I fancy it will some day come back into fashion. I believe that the quality it connotes is essential to all the arts. The stress and strain, the uncertainty of life in the past thirty years has not, I think, been favourable to the arts, though in those years a great deal of admirable work has of course been done (mostly, alas, by men of maturish years). Nor do I suppose that in my time, or until long after my time, will very propitious conditions supervene. There is a spate of planning for the future of many things. Perhaps some people are at this moment strenuously planning for the future of the arts. But I doubt whether in the equalitarian era for which we are heading—the era in which we shall have built Jerusalem on England's smooth and asphalt land —the art of literature, which throve so finely and so continuously from Elizabethan to paulo-post-Victorian days, will have a wonderful renascence. We are told on high authority, from both sides of the Atlantic, that the present century is to be the Century of the Common Man. We are all of us to go down on our knees and clasp our hands and raise our eyes and worship the Common Man. I am not a learned theologian, but I think I am right in saying that this religion has at least the hall-mark of novelty—has never before been propagated, even in the East, from which so many religions have sprung. Well, I am an old man, and old men are not ready converts to new religions. This one does not stir my soul. I take some comfort in the fact that its propagators do not seek to bind us to it for ever. " *This*," they say, "is to be the Century of the Common Man." I like to think that on the morning of January the first, in the year 2000, mankind will be free to unclasp its hands and rise from its knees and look about it for some other, and perhaps more rational, form of faith. I like also to think that in the meantime, in the great pale platitude of the meantime, there will be, as hitherto, a few discriminating readers of things written in past times; people likely to read, and likely to revel in, the works of Lytton Strachey. After all, it is always by the devotion of a few only that good books become classics.

I don't know whether it is "in order" to dedicate a Rede Lecture to anybody. If it is, I would like to dedicate this one to the memory of Lytton Strachey. I am always very proud that he dedicated one of his books, his last one, to me. Forgive me for boasting that he said "with gratitude and admiration." To him I dedicate this lecture with far greater gratitude than ever he can have felt to me, and with far deeper admiration than ever he can have had for anything of mine.

www.ingramcontent.com/pod-product-compliance
Ingram Content Group UK Ltd.
Pitfield, Milton Keynes, MK11 3LW, UK
UKHW042142280225
455719UK00001B/29